#FIRESTARTERS

HOW TO BE A SPARK OF HOPE
IN THE MIDST OF CHANGE

COLLECTION I

A Collection of Inspiring Stories from Creative Thought Leaders

www.selfpublishn30days.com

Copyright

Published by *Self Publish -N- 30 Days*

Copyright 2021 Shā Sparks, Sparks of Fire International, LLC

Printed in the United States of America

ISBN: 9-798-74832-559-2

1. Nonfiction 2. Self-Help 3. Motivational & Inspirational

Shā Sparks and Christine L Bowen *#FIRESTARTERS*

Contributing Authors: Adam Boubede, Alba Cordero Soto, Charli Caraway, David Bennett, Denise Duran, Joe Bogdan, & Moussa Mikhail

Disclaimer/Warning:

DEDICATION

For you, the creative thought leader, who sees the value in collaborating
while being the change you want to see.

ACKNOWLEDGMENTS

Profound Gratitude from the #FIRESTARTERS Book Project Co-Creators.

Thank you, God, for being the driving force that directed our steps with this project, in all of our relationships and in every conversation.

Thank you to each other for believing in each other and for being the true definition of a friend.

Thank you, Darren Palmer, for this incredible opportunity to create the #FIRESTARTERS Book Project. And for your exemplary leadership and friendship.

Thank you to the Self Publish -N- 30 Days team, Stephanie and Dr. Charli, for your guidance, grace, and hope.

Thank you to our mentors and coaches who continue to shape us to step into who we are divinely designed to be.

Last and certainly not least, thank you to each of the treasured co-authors for trusting yourselves, the process, and us. Thank you for your faith, leadership, courage, authenticity, and FIRE!

~ *Shā Sparks and Christine L Bowen*

TABLE OF

CONTENTS

Foreword – Darren M. Palmer 1

Introduction – Dr. Charli Caraway 5

Spark Your A.L.P.H.A. – Shā Sparks 11

The Chaos of Change – Christine L Bowen 21

Meaningful Change – Adam Boubede 31

An Eternal Light – Denise Duran 43

Better Has No Finish Line – Joe Bogdan 53

Be the Change – Alba Cordero Soto 65

Out of the Darkness – David Bennett 75

Life Teaches When We Listen – Moussa Mikhail 83

Conclusion 95

FOREWORD

BY DARREN M. PALMER

I met Shā several years ago, and from the moment we met, the instant connection created a spark that developed into a wonderful friendship and partnership. Through her, I have been able to connect with some of these amazing individuals that are a part of this book. In particular is Christine L Bowen. Christine has become a voice of inspiration to me and will for you as well.

As the Chief Book Officer of Self Publish -N- 30 Days, I have been blessed to work on several projects and conferences with Shā. Her inspiration and encouragement to help others are infectious. Once you meet her, you will never be the same.

I recall on social media when Shā Sparks shared about being a Firestarter — and how it all began with a spark. I instantly posed several questions. What does a Firestarter look like? What traits does a Firestarter embody? I wanted to make sure that I incorporated being a Firestarter like my dear friend, Shā. So when she asked me to write this foreword, I did not hesitate.

#FIRESTARTERS isn't a collection of placating stories designed to entertain you. It is a compilation of provoking, altering, and potentially dangerous excerpts that spark, or convict, the reader into change. Maybe you will change your perception. Maybe you will change your direction. But you will change.

After all, that's what a Firestarter is – a change agent. Within these pages, men and women have aligned themselves to share their greatness within. These authors have committed to carrying the flame that transfer thought into action.

1

The authors in this book saw opportunities that existed around them and their passion fueled them to take the first step, because all possibilities are wasted without action. They empower others to be better and seek out situations where their impact can be maximized. They disrupt or start things that most wouldn't. Their 'seize the moment' attitude changes the communities and the world around them.

What may have started as a small spark has set into motion flames of success, entrepreneurship, service, compassion, and life-changing perspectives. They have graduated from being the small, ineffectual ember forgotten in an old campfire.

They have allowed themselves to be stoked, moved, and fanned so that they are now firestarters – agents of change, spreading the consuming fire of passion for people.

Did you know the quantity and style of sparks produced from metals depends on the metal's composition and pyrophoricity? In the case of iron, the presence of carbon burns explosively in the hot iron and produces pretty, branching sparks.

The color of sparks used in pyrotechnics is determined by the material that the sparks are made from, with the possibility of adding different chemical compounds to certain materials to further influence the sparks' color. More reactive metals lead to hotter sparks.

These authors and their stories are tangible examples of this science. Each of them has proven to be a highly reactive metal that produces hot sparks. Each has had unique additives from their own life experiences that make their story unique.

I'm so excited that I have been able to glean from this team of fire-starting, change-invoking, power-stroking men and women. You will be glad you did as

well. A few things in these stories resonated with me. Everyone has the ability within themselves to create change. The drive for excellence is a lifestyle, not an outcome. Rather than being driven by results, each of these individuals consistently finds ways to keep their passion alive and well. This book will leave you with concrete inspiration for taking your life and setting it on fire.

Darren M. Palmer

Chief Book Officer

Self Publish -N- 30 Days

INTRODUCTION

BY DR. CHARLI CARAWAY

One of the great things about living in the country is the impromptu camping scenarios. To be more specific, campfires. Over the summer months, as limbs and natural debris are acquired and piled up for fall burning, it is fuel for the passion I have for cool weather, a cup of coffee, and a good sit-down as we burn.

Recently, we decided it was time for our first burn. As I was sitting and watching the fire, I received an amazing download, leadership, and life revelation that I'd like to share.

It begins with the way I started the fire. I use little fire starters that you buy at the local dollar store. You light those babies up and they burn for quite a while so that the limbs and debris that are around them have time to light and spread the flames. It occurred to me that some may call this cheating in the world of campfire builders, but I call it proper use of resources.

In fact, it reminded me that a fire starter is similar to a podcast, a motivational message, a book, or even a sermon that lights a fire under you. Maybe there is an event in your life or a revelation that occurs on a milestone birthday – but there's always that *thing* that lights your fire.

As that revelation hit me, I started studying fire differently. First, I considered how the fire spread. It wasn't the large limbs and logs that caught fire first. It was the small pieces, twigs, leaves, and pine straw. They caught the "vision" of the fire and assumed the fire the source was giving. It spread quickly amongst these small, insignificant pieces of yard debris and really carried the fire to the outer edges of the burn area. It was similar to the spread of a vision.

Next, I studied the growth of the fire. The more the small things lit up with flame, the more the larger things caught fire and began to burn. It occurred to me that once the larger pieces had begun to burn, there was less concern about the fire going out. Those larger pieces had a greater resource to keep the fire or the "vision" going. It was here that I recognized that both each part of the fire carried a responsibility, but neither was more important than the other.

I noticed as the fire began to strengthen and grow hotter, there was an ebb and flow to the flames. Sometimes it was hotter on one side of the fire or the flames were taller. Other times, the flames were dancing in the breeze and affecting the spread and strength of the burn.

My role in that fire was important. I realized that I needed to keep adding limbs and logs to the fire. It's similar when we've caught a vision. We have to keep feeding that vision. We must continually add fuel to the burning, the drive, so that the fire doesn't go out.

One of the things I've always noticed about campfires and bonfires is that after a while there are some really hot embers at the bottom. If you stoke those embers, they reignite and contribute greatly to the burning process overall. Isn't that what mentors and leaders do for us? Isn't that why we listen to motivational messages and read materials that inspire us? It stokes our fire!

One of my favorite parts about fires, especially outdoor fires, are the ashes. Eventually, those tiny pieces of debris turn to ash and the slightest breeze will begin to lift them and carry them off. I think it's beautiful. However, this particular evening, it occurred to me that those ashes, still hot, have the potential to land somewhere else and carry the fire. They have the potential to take the vision and spread it. The logs and large limbs do not. They can't be counted on for movement, but the ashes can.

The other relevant point about the ashes is that they may not light up a fire when they land, but the ash is filled with the nutrients and minerals of the materials they came from and they provide fertilizer and replenish the soil on which they fall. So, it doesn't matter if they're hot with the "vision" of the fire or if they've cooled. They still have the core elements of the fire within them to supply other parts of the earth with their goodness.

Recently, it rained for several days. Because of this, only the debris on the top of my little mountain of limbs from the summer months was dry. After a while, I started getting to limbs and debris that were still wet. When I put them on the fire, the fire started to smoke. At one point, it seemed that the flames were dissipating, and the fire might go out. It reminded me of the negativity we encounter when we are sharing a vision.

Dry debris catches quickly because it is depleted of moisture and able to serve a purpose. However, wet debris is filled with moisture, like preconceived ideas and opinions based on past experiences, which can be like water on your fire. However, a well-fed (motivated) and well-tended (purposeful and intentional) fire can burn off the moisture in the wet debris. It separates itself from any negativity that would put out the fire and prevent its spread.

What a beautiful concept that a small, insignificant flame can bring so much revelation and understanding about the human process. Don't let your flame die. Tend it. Feed it. Observe it. Respect its process. And most of all, enjoy how it heats and lights up an otherwise dark world!

MEET
CHARLI CARAWAY

Dr. Charli Caraway, better known as 'Dr. Charli the Book Mama' (#drcharlithebookmama) is the CEO of Rapha Alliance, a coaching and writing company training individuals for personal improvement. A speaker, life coach, writer, and editor, Dr. Charli speaks and teaches coast to coast. She loves to 'keep it real' with humor in leadership and personal development which has gained her the recognition of being a 'velvet hammer'. You can catch her on her weekly Facebook Live called "Writer's Therapy," with her amazing co-host, 'The Grammar Queen.'

With a BA in Communications and Technical Documentation, MA in Secondary Education and in Educational Administration, and an EdD in Educational Leadership, Dr. Charli has a range of experience to make writing and speaking valuable and fun. Her resumé spans small business, corporate leadership, public and private education, university teaching and administration, consulting, and non-profit management.

Dr. Charli believes in empowering people and has given her time to many community organizations which includes serving the homeless and impoverished communities, broken families, and the elderly. She's even served as an official Wish Granter for the Make-A-Wish Foundation. Currently, she serves as the Vice President of Public Relations for Aglow International North Central Texas Area, and is on the Board of Directors for Active-Faith.

She and her husband Rodney live in East Texas somewhere between the chickens, the cows, and the oil derricks. They have four adult children and two beautiful dogs. When they aren't working, they love to travel, cook southern and Cajun cuisine, or go camping.

You can find Dr. Charli at drcharlic@gmail.com or LinkedIn.

SPARK YOUR A.L.P.H.A.

BY SHĀ SPARKS

"You could work with veterans," he said to me when I first met him and asked about my coaching business geared toward transforming trauma into treasure. He didn't know all the events leading up to that moment.

Have you ever noticed how patterns show up in your life? It could be that everyone is driving the same color car or when you keep meeting people from a specific group. I started to notice a pattern showing up in my life. For several years, I would be meeting people who had some sort of military experience. I would go to business-related networking events, meet lots of people, and sure enough, I would meet someone with a military background.

Now, that may not be a big deal to you. But for me, it sparked a question that kept swirling in my mind. Does this pattern of military veterans and personnel crossing my path mean something? It is my belief that everything happens for a reason. Therefore, I pay attention when patterns show up and ask myself, "What is the purpose of this happening?" Analyzing the process of what's going on allows me to get clarity on a reason why something is happening. I believe patterns are God's way of grabbing our attention. Patterns will continue to show up until we start taking action. Sometimes, we are required to take action that is completely out of our comfort zones.

YEARS BEFORE THIS

Let me take you back to where my journey began in a verbally, physically, and emotionally abusive relationship. Unfortunately, my former boyfriend behaved how he was treated as a child. Don't get me wrong. I get that we all have a choice, and he could have chosen not to be an abuser himself; however, I don't think he knew that he had that choice. I don't believe he had the tools to be a better person. Once I got out of that relationship, I was determined to find my own tools to prevent repeating that abusive relationship. I knew that I needed help; however, I had no idea what I was going to learn.

PATTERNS WILL CONTINUE TO SHOW UP UNTIL WE START TAKING ACTION.

After starting therapy within the first week of being away from this man, I found myself saying that I didn't have a choice; I had to stay and take care of him. Later on, I learned that my brain had switched over from me being in a relationship with a potential spouse to being in a parent-child relationship. Consequently, the thought of leaving him made me feel guilty, as if I were a mother abandoning her child. How could I possibly choose to abandon him? I felt I didn't have a choice. He thought he needed me and that I had to take care of him. I had tried to break up with him before, yet he was able to craft incredibly touching stories to manipulate my heartstrings, and my nurturing "mother" brain would kick in and take over.

Ultimately, the choice to leave him was made for me. Due to a car accident, he was in a coma with a brain injury. Basically, I was able to slowly walk away and let his family know what had been going on up until then. Even though it was extremely difficult, I made the right decision for me. I needed to focus on healing myself. I needed to make better choices in relationships, in my business, and for myself.

After a few months of healing, a pattern showed up of women who shared their stories of abuse with me. Fueled with a new desire to positively guide them, I shared what I had learned from my own experience and spoke to them in a way that I wished someone had spoken to me when I was in my abusive relationship. It worked! They each made the choice to move towards healing and to choose better relationships.

TRAUMA: STRESS INTO GROWTH MINDSET

For several years, I researched information on the brain, the effects of trauma, and how it will show up years later. One thing I learned is that trauma results from an experience that happened, and as we know, we can't change the experience. However, more importantly, is that even years later, the effect it has on the brain can be shifted. We must learn how our brain interprets the experience. Each person's brain is as unique as the individual it belongs to, like our fingerprints. How each person's brain interprets an experience will be unique. No test exists to know for sure what will work for each person to pull themselves out of trauma. It is all trial and error to find out what works best for each person.

A few years later, I was interviewing an EMT/firefighter, who had also been in the National Guard, for my podcast. He explained that he had been diagnosed with post-traumatic stress disorder (PTSD) from his career experiences, including being involved in the Oklahoma City bombing recovery. He had gone through various things to recover, including equine therapy. This was when everything I learned in my own trauma recovery started to click.

As a society, we typically use the term PTSD in association with only military background experiences. However, I saw it in the domestic violence survivors that I talked with. I saw it in someone who had an abortion. I saw it in people who have lost their children, and I saw it in people who had been in a horrific car accident. I saw it in those who had experienced combat situations.

All these stories became a pattern to me, and their experiences all shuffled around in my brain, along with my own experience. That's when I had an ah-ha moment – *we have all experienced some sort of trauma if our brain interprets it that way.* Although we cannot choose how our brain interprets that experience, we can choose how we move forward. We can choose to change the narrative from post-traumatic stress to post-traumatic growth. I realized that I had taken my personal traumatic journey and transformed my life and my business into a treasure. When I shared my story, not only did I heal more, I was able to inspire others to heal.

GROWING UP

As children, we often see how our parents treat each other and glean how we are to be treated in a relationship. Childhood is where we first learn how to love and what love looks like. We only know what we see, hear, and experience for ourselves. Our brains process this information as a model for what love looks like. Unless we experience and understand that there are many different ways people show love, we only know what we know.

If we only know what we know, we believe that to be true for everyone and everything. For example, if you grew up in a household where dad worked outside the home and mom stayed home, when you grow up, you might have the same roles in your marriage. Even though you don't realize it, that dynamic is what you are used to seeing. The same goes for abuse. If you're used to seeing mom get abused by dad, more than likely, your brain will believe that's how life is supposed to be. If your parents go to college, you believe you must go to college. The same goes for being in the military. If you don't actively see that you have a choice to do something

WE HAVE ALL EXPERIENCED SOME SORT OF TRAUMA IF OUR BRAIN INTERPRETS IT THAT WAY.

different, then you will choose to do what you're accustomed to seeing.

During my own childhood, I saw my mom sad and unhappy most of the time. She and my dad fought, she went from being sad to being depressed to being bitter. I remember asking her if she ever thought about getting a divorce and she said, "What would I do?" Looking back at that conversation, I now see she did not believe that she had any other choice but to stay with my dad. As for my dad, he never talked about his time in the military. On occasion, he would show me black-and-white pictures of him in his army fatigues. He would not share what happened during his time in Korea. He did have this beautiful quilt that he brought back from when he was stationed there. Today, that quilt is in my guest bedroom as a beautiful reminder of my dad.

Six months before he died, (Of course, I didn't know that at the time. I wish I had asked him more about it during those months) Dad shared with my brother and me that he was drafted by a lottery system to be deployed to Korea from the Army Reserves. When he did share, he said something that resonated deeper than anything else he's ever said to me.

As he told his story, he described being a farm kid shipped off to the military and not knowing what to do. "I didn't have a choice," he said. That particular phrase hung in the air as if I was reading a comic strip, and it had its own thought bubble circling it.

That phrase stayed with me and sunk into my heart. I realized there was a period of my life where I didn't feel like I had a choice. A year after he passed, I was talking to another veteran and he shared that he goes to Walter Reed Hospital to treat his PTSD and would prefer to have his appointments via Skype or Zoom. Then he said those same words that sounded like brakes on a car that came to a screeching halt. Not only did my ears and brain hear those same words, my soul screamed to attention. He said, "But I don't have a choice."

I DON'T HAVE A CHOICE EXCEPT TO SUCCEED

What I have learned over the years from my passion for studying trauma and the brain is that fear is how our brain interprets the traumatic experience(s) we have. Fear creates a story to keep us safe, to protect us. Fear keeps us safe by keeping us in our comfort zone and will show up when we try something new and/or when something reminds our brain of any traumatic experience, whether recent or long ago.

> **I BEGAN TO ASK THE QUESTION, "WHAT LIGHTS YOUR SOUL ON FIRE?"**

Personally, fear had stopped me from doing and achieving many things. Once I recognized that, I began the journey of stepping out of my comfort zone on a regular basis. It's been a lot of fun, a lot of work, a lot of risks, and it's been worth every single scary step. A few risks I've taken include pitching a software idea at Start-Up Weekend, taking improv classes, training in Krav Maga, attending the Country Music Awards, traveling the U.S. alone, getting certified in Social Entrepreneurship, starting a podcast, and becoming a Certified Fearless Living Coach.

I am sharing my experiences with you so that if you're saying to yourself, "I can't do something out of my comfort zone," I'm living proof that you can! If you are willing to shift your stress mindset from "I don't have a choice" to "I can grow," you might just be able to say, "I don't have a choice except to succeed."

SPARK YOUR A.L.P.H A.

"Alpha" popped into my head so loud, it woke me from my sleep in the middle of the night. I knew instantly that this was an extremely important word. The next morning while journaling, I took a moment and asked God, what does "alpha" mean? As fast as I could write, the message I received was that it was an acronym for the words Awareness, Leadership, Purpose, Hope, and Alignment. I began exploring what this acronym was for and for whom.

At first, I thought it was for the women's empowerment workshop for which I was planning my message. I thought my purpose was to empower women to start businesses. However, after hearing that I could work with veterans, and learning from veterans that there was a disconnect for them as they transitioned from military life to civilian life, I changed my trajectory.

Veterans are not encouraged to find their purpose post-military. They had been given a purpose by the military and now it is up to them to figure out the rest. I began to ask the question, "What lights your soul on fire?" After talking with many people from various military and non-military backgrounds, only a few felt like they had taken time to find their purpose. For most, it wasn't even something they thought about.

That is how Spark Your A.L.P.H.A. became a coaching program. First, we spark your self-Awareness and the opportunities around you. Second, we spark your Leadership skills so that you communicate more intentionally to lead with your heart as well as your head. Third, we spark your Purpose so you feel more excited about your life and business. Fourth, we spark Hope into your life to proactively manage fear when it shows up. Last but not least, we bring it all together with a more passionate and purposeful Alignment. When we stoke the internal fire that burns inside each veteran, they have more clarity on what fearless actions to take next. That action can be to start a business or non-profit, write a book, or coach others.

Spark Your A.L.P.H.A. empowers veterans and those thinking about becoming a small business owner to step out of their comfort zone, re-ignite their passion into a more aligned purpose, and transform it into increased profits and personal growth. In addition, they experience a higher level of emotional intelligence, awareness, and gratitude that allows them to lead from their heart and head.

Now, jumping ahead to the day my life would shift in ways I never imagined. When I was at a podcast conference and a gentleman I met suggested, "You could work with veterans," he had no idea about the pattern of veterans in my life or that I had written a speech for a women's empowerment event around the word "alpha." Nor did he fathom that I was creating a coaching course where the first step was to be aware of the opportunities around you. In that brief 20-minute conversation, he was simply suggesting that I work with veterans based on my tag line of Transforming Trauma into Treasure. What he actually did was confirm what was right in front of me and inside of me.

Personally, I knew from the age of 19 that I was on this planet to make a positive impact on other people's lives. I believe God gave me the answer to transforming post-traumatic stress into growth.

Just recently, I realized how my soul gets fired up with excitement when I see others use the obstacles they have faced and transform those experiences into a treasure when they acknowledge their own resiliency.

In conclusion, I leave you with this to ponder: What lights and excites your soul on fire?

MEET
SHĀ SPARKS

Growing up with a father who was unwillfully drafted in the Army to serve time in Korea, Shā inherited her father's "I don't have a choice" mindset. Later she realized she did have a choice and overcame abuse, addiction, depression, anger, low self-worth, being a bully, and being bullied. Today, she has proactively changed that fear-based phrase "I don't have a choice" into determination, inspiring others to make fearless choices. She knows that if she can take her own traumatic experiences and transform them into a treasure, then so can you!

Shā is the CEO (Chief Excitement Officer) of Sparks of Fire International, LLC, a Certified Fearless Living Coach, host of The Power of Investing in People podcast, host of "Hey Shā, What Do I Say?" Facebook Live show, author of "How to Get Your Voice Back," and Co-Founder of #FIRESTARTERS Book Project. As a business coach, author, podcast host, and speaker, she guides leaders to re-ignite their passion into a more aligned purpose and transform it into increased profit.

"When we share our own lessons learned of overcoming obstacles, we ignite a tiny spark of hope, love, connection, and community. And when we ignite that spark, the whole world lights up. That's *The Power of Investing in People!*"

You may find out more about her other books, podcast, and other resources at her website www.shasparks.com or email heysha@shasparks.com

THE CHAOS OF CHANGE

BY CHRISTINE L BOWEN

At the beginning of 2020, it was not my intention to be writing these words for public consumption. *I had other plans for 2020!* Sound familiar? One of my favorite quotes comes by way of a Yiddish proverb, *"We Plan, God Laughs."* Religious dogma aside, you have to chuckle with this quote simply because it rings loud and true. How many times have you made plans that turned out an entirely different way, if at all?

2020.

Regardless of any and all differences, this generation of our human race has one thing in common – and that is this year called 2020. Initially, 2020 was a special New Year – it was the turn of a new decade! Most, if not all, of us approached 2020 with wide-eyed enthusiasm, renewed zeal, and a vision bigger than life itself. In my circles, there were declarations of taking that leap of faith, starting that new business, meeting that new mate, going back to school. Oh, the lists continue, right? Whatever the vision, we were ready to live our best lives. Then, in what seemed like an instant, life changed – impacting every person across the globe. Year 2020 pulled a Dr. Jekyll and Mr. Hyde – our New Year now appeared to be our New Nightmare.

In stark contrast to our expectations, and completely outside the scope of what any of us had ever imagined, we have found ourselves in the midst of the biggest global shift in human history. We are facing individual and collective challenges on an unprecedented scale. Fear and uncertainty are so palpable they could be dubbed actual beings. And here we are, with no choice but to deal with all of it.

Interestingly, Change is not new to us. History has demonstrated time and again that the human race has the innate ability to not only evolve but also innovate and create, especially during times of intense change. Yet, even though we are familiar with "change," it certainly presents us with new challenges each time it arrives at our doorstep. 2020 is no different; at the same time, it's completely different. In the blink of an eye, every aspect of life, as we knew it, has forever changed.

Our way of living changed.

Our way of communicating changed.

Our way of doing business changed.

Our way of educating changed.

Everything changed!

So much changed that even our understanding of Change is changing—all declarations made at the beginning of 2020, shattered in one fell swoop. Summed up, if you look up the word change in the dictionary, chaos would be the primary definition.

Dr. Deepak Chopra, MD, my long-time mentor and spiritual guide, often says, "All great changes are preceded by chaos." Sounds good, right? But is it too good to be true? Are we to believe that something great is around the bend, beyond the compounding crisis that appears to be our present reality?

Circling back to writing this chapter, when my dear divine connection, Shā Sparks, approached me with this brilliant idea to create the #FIRESTARTERS movement, my first inclination was to decline. Our desire to collaborate with each other was six years in the making, yet I was about to pass on this incredible opportunity! The timeframe was early May of 2020; we were about two-plus months into the pandemic, and I was NOT handling the situation well. Resistance stepped right in saying ...

Is this the right time to start something new?

This is not what I had planned for 2020!

I'm not even a writer!

Oh, Resistance carried on! Although change was a concept that I embraced over a decade ago, the level of change that 2020 brought into our life's scope shook me to the core, punched me in the gut, and dropped me flat on my butt. I felt anxious, angry, depressed, helpless, frustrated, and isolated.

Being a long-time practitioner of personal and spiritual development, one would think my adeptness for navigating life's constant changes would be a cinch. However, both you and I know that life's never-ending curveballs hit differently pretty much every single time. Thankfully, we have resilience on our side. Yet, even the most practiced was not ready to handle the level of change that 2020 has ushered into all of our lives. Every aspect of my faith and resilience has been challenged. At one point, my attempts to *"Vibrate Higher"* felt like they were useless. For the first time in my life, I was alone, and I was straight-up scared.

True to form, my absolute faith activated my higher consciousness. Clarity revealed that my high resistance was a clear indication that my mind was mired in fear. My creative mind was clouded by the intensity of my lower vibrations. 2020 had kicked me into default mode. I can surely say my faith and resilience were being tested through the fire of Change.

Within the same moment, I was thinking about turning down this incredible opportunity, my higher Self whispered to me ...

EVERY ASPECT OF MY FAITH AND RESILIENCE HAS BEEN CHALLENGED.

You've been here before.

Let's disconnect so you can reconnect.

Let's quiet your mind so you can hear what 2020 has to say.

In the blink of an eye, it became apparent to me that, although destructive in so many ways, 2020 is actually here to teach us some very valuable lessons and remind us of certain things that will provide the Hope we all desperately need right now.

Rather than partake in the thick of the chaos, I made a conscious decision to invest most of my time reflecting on the meaning of 2020's chain of events and the lessons life is teaching us at this moment in time.

While there are *many* lessons, I am selecting a few that 2020 has brought to the forefront of my consciousness. Here are just a few of the hundreds of lessons I've learned:

LIFE LESSON SELECTION #137 – CHANGE FORTIFIES

My relationship with Change began at a very tender age. I was around eight years old when my parents' marriage ended. My mother moved us from our home base in NYC back to our homeland, Jamaica. Prior to moving, I was in Jamaica as much as I was in the States. Living there full-time was an entirely different experience. Imagine the culture shock – especially for a young child – going from color television to black and white; from air-conditioned homes to open windows and year-round heat; from relatively safe US suburbs to a country riddled with violent crime, from a little girl to growing up too soon.

With that said, I wouldn't trade my upbringing for anything. There is a Jamaican proverb you will hear our people chanting far and wide, *"We likkle, but we tallawah!"*, meaning *"We are small, but we are mighty!"* Regardless of circumstance, we stand firm on faith and resiliency to conquer any and all of life's challenges.

The first time I recall being formally introduced to Change was on September 12, 1988. A few days earlier, all eyes were on Hurricane Gilbert as it barreled across the Atlantic Ocean. It was on a clear path to our tiny island, and we were bracing ourselves for its Cat 5, 185 mph winds. Gilbert struck land on the eastern tip of Jamaica on the morning of September 12 and, by nightfall, had traveled clear across to the western tip, leaving massive destruction in its wake. Our beautiful country was destroyed! Although clearly an ordeal, it wasn't the storm itself that brought me eye-to-eye with Change that day; it was a certain moment that awakened me to how powerful we are in the midst of adversity.

It was around mid-afternoon; Gilbert had already stripped most of our neighbors' homes of their rooftops and we were simply counting down for our turn. The power was already out, and the wind and rain were relentless. Suddenly, it was raining in our bedrooms! Without hesitation, my mother and I sprang into action.

Two women of petite stature cleared out two rooms of furniture et al within nanoseconds! The upper foyer was so jam-packed we had to climb over the pile to get to my Mom's master bedroom, turned panic room.

Shortly after, the eye of the storm reached our city of Kingston, and we all ventured outside to survey the damage. Miraculously, our roof was still intact. The wind had lifted the roof just enough for the rain to blow under the eave. As I stood there in shock and gratitude, what had occurred moments before came rushing back to me.

Where on Earth did I muster up that kind of strength?

How did we move all those things and fit them into a small foyer?

"WE LIKKLE, BUT WE TALLAWAH!"

> **I FELT LIKE CHANGE CAME INTO TOWN TO BEAT ME DOWN AND LEAVE ME FOR DEAD.**

Why was our roof preserved and not the homes to the left or right of us?

In the wake of Chaos, I discovered the wisdom of Change. That experience, as harrowing as it was, introduced me to a kind of strength I never realized I possessed. Certainly, adrenaline plays a role. However, upon deeper reflection of why we are designed to function in this way, it provides us with the understanding and fortitude to push through challenging times. It lends itself to the evidence and presence of a Power Source much stronger than us, one that fuels us, one that promotes creative and solution-oriented thinking, one that fuels action rather than stagnation – especially so during adverse times.

Today, I am reminded that this same Power Source is inexhaustible, present, and available for both you and me in 2020 and beyond.

LIFE LESSONS SELECTION #245 – CHANGE CLARIFIES

At the turn of the last decade, I embarked upon a journey of self-discovery, which opened the door to my spiritual awakening. Even though I was a student in a religious sense for many years, this was my first time exploring my spirituality independently. Fundamental truths were being revealed that answered many of my life-long questions and opened my eyes to my purpose for being on this Earth.

These revelations initiated a series of bold changes I created for my life. I walked away from a six-figure income as an employee to resume my full-time career as a creative entrepreneur. I stretched myself into new arenas of professional networking and media broadcasting. Lastly, the boldest move of all, after several years of denial, I finally accepted that my long-term relationship had come to the point of dissolution, and I decided to start over on my own.

Although each decision was made with great consideration and trepidation, I put my big toe over the fear line, and I did it afraid. With so much change, I was shaken, but not stirred. I was conscious of where I was in life and the direction in which I was headed. I was in creative control of my life and started 2018 with confidence.

Little did I know, Change was waiting for me around the corner.

In February of 2018, I was offered the contract of a lifetime. A new client collaborator wanted to retain my services on an on-going basis. The starting compensation was four figures per month, and I was on a high. My new year and my new life were off to a fantastic start!

The very next day after signing the contract, I woke up to blurred vision. I could not see anything clearly – near or far. This was a major crisis for a graphic designer who was also ridesharing to make ends meet.

Am I going blind?

How am I going to maintain my bills?

I just signed this contract!

I was rendered still, speechless, and scared shitless! I didn't know what was wrong, but I knew enough to know that Change had come to pay me a visit. The blurred vision was only the beginning. The following month, my father, who had never been sick in his entire life, was severely ill, relationships that I had built for many years were falling apart, my professional presence I spent years growing was losing credibility, and by mid-year I was exhausted. I felt like Change came into town to beat me down and leave me for dead.

Concurrently with these events, I was on a mission to discover *why*.

Why was life giving me a beat-down?

What was I missing?

I felt so defeated.

When Life is ready to teach us a lesson, Change enters the picture to clarify the message. The longer we allow Resistance to play its role, the more chaotic life becomes. It continues sending signals until conditions get to the point that we have no choice but to pay attention. It is during that crucial window of time that we are presented with the priceless opportunity to slow down just enough to look outside of ourselves to the bigger picture.

These moments of Change reveal to us how our thoughts and actions, or lack thereof, affect our reality and that of the world at large. Change reveals to us that while we are in control of our micro-world, if our actions are not in alignment with the harmony of the Universe, then our charted course will only lead to frustration. Being willing to surrender to the Wisdom of Universal Harmony is one of the biggest lessons that Change continues to teach me.

LIFE LESSON SELECTION #308 – CHANGE REFINES

This lesson is happening in real-time. Thus far, Change has clearly shown me that 2020 is a year of refinement, not just for me, but for all of us. Refinement is defined as the process of removing impurities or unwanted elements from a substance. Now that I've regained clarity, it has become apparent to me that the chain of events leading up to this point brought to the surface many deep-rooted traumas that I was blind to before. I am beginning to understand that bypassing the pain of the past doesn't heal them, and 2020 has surely come to reveal them. Change is teaching me that with my light comes darkness, and true change is found in our willingness to face and embrace our darkness. In doing so, we shine even brighter – individually and collectively.

This is the greatness Dr. Chopra is referring to in his quote. Greatness is not an event; greatness is not around the bend; greatness is right here, right NOW. Greatness is YOU, and greatness is ME. And together, WE will CREATE the CHANGE we wish to see in this world.

Together, we are #FIRESTARTERS!

MEET
CHRISTINE L BOWEN (CLB)

Christine L Bowen (CLB) is a free-spirited conscious creative who lives presently, loves wholeheartedly, laughs regularly, and is extremely passionate about living life at its creative best and inspiring others to enjoy the same.

With over 30 years of combined experience in the areas of visual communication, professional networking, and mass media, CLB is dedicated to serving fellow heart-centered professionals who desire to achieve a higher level of excellence with their brand identity & social presence. Her unique approach inspires you to infuse greater consciousness, connection, and creativity into your TOTAL presence.

When collaborating with CLB, she liberates you from the frustration and limitation of status quo standards and restores you to your natural, peaceful state of conscious creation. You are empowered to intuitively attract and align with ideal people and opportunities, creating a more sustainable, thriving, fulfilling business – and life!

CLB currently resides in Washington D.C. and is pursuing her PhD in Conscious Centered Living.

You're invited to connect with her at www.ChristineLBowen.com.

MEANINGFUL CHANGE

BY ADAM BOUBEDE

The best part of being an instigator of change is working towards building something better. When we make the decision to initiate change, we must first consider if it is meaningful. We should seek to connect our idea for change to a greater purpose with the goal of improving the lives of others or helping an organization create more value for its members. This is a chronicle of my journey of finding purpose and putting it to work.

"The meaning of life is to find your gift. The purpose of life is to give it away."
- Pablo Picasso

WHERE I FOUND MY SPARK AND HOW YOU CAN START YOUR OWN!

My spark came to me when I found a way to amplify my WHY. Have you taken the time to figure out your own WHY? Learning about purpose-driven leadership can help you. This is the concept that helped me grow as a leader and allowed me to find my WHY, which is to build developmental environments and create conditions for meaningful work where every person can discover their own purpose and become the best version of themselves.

This journey led me to find the Society of American Military Engineers (SAME), an organization that leads collaboration among government and industry to develop multi-disciplined solutions to national security

> ## MY SPARK CAME TO ME WHEN I FOUND A WAY TO AMPLIFY MY WHY.

infrastructure challenges. I learned about SAME in 2010. However, my initial impression was that it did not have anything of value to offer a young noncommissioned officer.

"A leader's job is to look into the future and see the organization, not as it is, but as it should be."

– Jack Welch

Fast forward four years to 2014 when a good friend helped me see what they truly had to offer and convinced me to become a member of the organization. This was a pivotal moment of unforeseen opportunity, and my career path changed for the better by committing myself to work with SAME. This taught me why it is important that we fully explore every opportunity before completely dismissing them. The sooner that we realize how to take the time to learn about an opportunity, the more equipped we are to avoid misjudging them so that we do not miss our moment to grow in a new direction.

"Courageous leaders are those who would rather challenge what needs to be changed and pay the price than remain silent and slowly die inside."

– Andy Stanley

Finding an organization with overwhelming value to offer through networking, professional development, and leadership opportunities propelled my success. Unfortunately, this non-profit, founded in 1920, traditionally did not have a large, enlisted membership, and enlisted service members only accounted for approximately 1% of more than 29,000 members. This scarcity was further evident as I routinely found myself solely representing the enlisted force when attending SAME events. I felt, as an enlisted member who was benefiting from being a part of the organization, that this was unacceptable and needed to change so that more enlisted members could benefit from the same opportunities I had been afforded. However, I quickly learned that this reality was not the intention of the organization's leaders, so I took the initiative to develop a better communication plan for the Society.

Speaking with fellow enlisted service members made it apparent they were not convinced of the value that the organization had to offer. This taught us that it was not enough to simply *tell* them it existed; we had to be an example of how beneficial the organization was to generate personal and professional growth. Ultimately, we needed to *show* them.

"The secret of change is to focus all of your energy,
NOT on fighting the old, but on building the new."

– Socrates

With the world in front of me, I had to make a choice: wait for something to happen or take action. I chose to make that change happen, so I sought out other passionate enlisted members, and together we decided to embark on an effort to organize a new movement that would serve as a focal point to broadcast the value of SAME's message. We knew that the only way anything would change or that any progress would be made was to become the change we wanted to see. We decided to form an Enlisted Committee in order to advocate for change across the organization with the goal of creating and delivering meaningful value for others. To generate interest, we started monthly teleconference calls, developed a new value brief with a marketing plan, and teamed up with leaders of the 105 SAME posts worldwide to build outreach programs for enlisted members.

CREATING A CONDUIT FOR CONNECTING PEOPLE

"A leader delivers results through people."

– Raja Gopaal Tyer

Our initiative paid off! In less than two years, this committee grew into a diverse 17-member team with representatives from every U.S. military service branch. Shortly afterward, the Enlisted Committee earned a seat on SAME's National

Board of Direction and successfully initiated many ideas, including veteran transition programs, awards programs, STEM programs, and input into the development of a five-year National Strategic Plan. This journey taught me patience, that change takes time, and that rushing objectives can create a failed outcome. By taking our time to build a good foundation, we were able to establish a sound structure to propel our success. It is worth adding that since the inception of the Enlisted Committee, SAME membership and active participation by enlisted members have more than tripled and continue to grow each year.

HOW YOU CAN FUEL YOUR FIRE!

After you have found your spark and ignited your fire, you need to find fuel to keep it burning bright. Plainly said, you need to gather resources that feed your pursuit and help you reach your goals.

LOOK TO YOURSELF AND UNDERSTAND THE SOURCES OF POWER YOU HAVE WITHIN YOUR CONTROL.

First, look to yourself and understand the sources of power you have within your control, such as position, expertise, wealth, and social connections. However, nothing is more incredibly powerful than your own passion for pursuing your goals. To fully leverage this ability, it is imperative that you are actively involved and make consistent progress towards your goals. Simply put, your actions speak louder than your words, and consistency outmatches intensity. Much like routinely throwing a log onto a fire, know that it is easier to make progress and build momentum by contributing an hour every week towards your goal versus four hours for a single day in a month. Now you just need to communicate what you are working towards.

I FOUND MY JUST CAUSE

This is where you transform your passion into action! Pouring effort into something you are passionate about transforms your work into a rewarding pursuit of your goal. Teaming with SAME unlocked its resources to fuel my passion for developing others. In his book *Infinite Game*, Simon Sinek explains that a just cause is "a specific vision of a future state that does not exist; a future state so appealing that people are willing to make sacrifices in order to help advance toward that vision." Using this principle, the vision I created became: "Every Engineer, Every Service, Know SAME." It is simple, it has no end state, and it can build upon itself indefinitely. This is the idea that gave our initiative direction and kept all of our actions on course. The intent is to leverage every communication medium available to showcase the value of SAME to every military engineer, both officer and enlisted. I saw how much this organization could empower others to do great things, and I was driven to make that vision a reality.

"You never change things by fighting the existing reality. To change something, build a new model that makes the existing model obsolete."

– Buckminster Fuller

I realized that the benefits which accompany working towards this vision are immeasurable. We envisioned the potential for growth through increased membership in the Society and took every opportunity to share these ideas with others. The added benefit was that investing in this change helped me invest in the people I work with every day.

More specifically, forming professional relationships and building connections expanded the resources that were available for me to grow and develop my fellow noncommissioned officers. The overall message that we sought to communicate was that we must invest in the growth of our enlisted force to truly build a better future and a strong-willed force full of equally well-equipped leaders.

NETWORKING AND BUILDING A TRIBE

"If you want to go fast, go alone. If you want to go far, go together."

– African Proverb

Know that you cannot accomplish your goal alone, so networking will quickly become the resource that has the greatest potential for the largest yield on a return investment or effort and time. A strong team will help everyone work less yet accomplish more, so it is critical that you understand the importance of collaboration while inspiring others to join the fight to promote the goal.

Good collaboration exists when the relationship creates value for both parties and helps in accomplishing the goal, so you must build a shared value proposition to rally others with a strong and clear message. I learned how to leverage my passion to recruit others and to build motivation for them by creating a shared vision. When reaching out, remember to act for the benefit of others before you act for yourself. It is vital to understand that networking is about relationships, and the bonds you build with others are strengthened by the quality of that relationship.

"The more you give to others, the more you get back."

– Logan, King, Fischer-Wright: *Tribal Leadership*

When you begin networking, start with what you can give them and **not** what they can provide for you. Take the time to listen to them and learn about their needs first. Imagine that they have no benefit to offer you. This is a safe position to start from and will help you listen to their needs to see what you can offer to them.

As you develop the relationship, your new network will begin to reveal hidden benefits. Know that people connect through relationships, and you need to invest in this concept by building meaningful relationships. As you progress, your connections will likely gain interest in you and your idea, and they will then spread your idea to others. After all, team successes are more enduring and satisfying because they are shared.

HOW TO KEEP YOUR FIRE ALIVE!

"Who you are precedes what you do."

– Simon Sinek

Your message is important, but so is your character. When rallying others to your cause, they need to trust you before they trust your ideas. Know that your presence and involvement at all levels of an organization are absolutely essential to driving change. The better your audience knows and understands your values, the more willing they will be to follow your lead. In order for your idea to endure and continue growing, you need to protect it by gaining support from others. It is a good practice to have your message ready to deliver at all times. This will help you to gather additional resources to strengthen your goals in planned and unplanned settings.

"Don't trust rules, trust people."

– Simon Sinek

Remember that you need to remain committed to the change while refusing to let minor setbacks halt your efforts. Do not be dissuaded by current organizational structures that block your way. You must work to break through the barriers that are blocking your resources or find a way around them. Realistically, barriers can become opportunities to improve your idea, increase your network, and gain new perspectives.

This moment came for us when we were seeking a charter with the National Board of Direction for our Enlisted Committee. Our initial plan for the Enlisted Committee was to only invite enlisted service members to be a part of it because that is who we are and who we serve. However, SAME's national leadership team saw little value in a purely demographics-based group. When faced with this obstacle, we chose to use it to empower our cause. Remembering the goal of creating value for others, we modified our proposition to read that any person who is willing to support the values of our newly-founded committee is welcome to join and take part.

You need to grow the capacity in yourself to face your dissenters. Take the time to learn their perspectives and incorporate their views to turn them into supporters. You need to be willing to have uncomfortable conversations with those who have opposing views on the issues that you are seeking to address in your change initiative. While challenging, much can be gained by learning to see through the lens of another person.

By putting yourself in their shoes, you may learn that you need to shift the direction of your plan of action. And while accepting the validity of conflicting ideas can be tough, you should embrace it to see the underlying value. Doing so helped us instantly build diversity and increased our pool of membership.

Additionally, you must not fear taking risks as adversity is what drives growth. View your obstacles as potential rather than barriers to your success.

The best plan for the future viability of your idea and vision requires timely succession planning to position the right people in leadership roles. Ultimately, you want your idea to be enduring. After all, a flash in the pan pales in comparison to a raging inferno, but you cannot carry the torch forever, nor should you.

ULTIMATELY, YOU WANT YOUR IDEA TO BE ENDURING.

At some point, you will need to pass on the torch to someone else. This might be the most difficult thing that you do, so I implore you to be deliberate about building a succession plan. Doing so is more than simply picking a protégé. You need to find someone with a similar passion

38

for the values you established and trust them to lead the way. Finally, find the courage in yourself to step back and support them as they take control of what you created and help it grow. Be a mentor for them and become a dedicated fuel source for their fire.

"Leadership is about making others better as a result of your presence

and making sure that impact lasts in your absence."

- Sheryl Sandberg, COO of Facebook

This journey taught me many lessons, and now I know that everything starts with finding your purpose and discovering your inner passions. I discovered that dedicating effort toward what we are passionate about does not feel like work. It tends to feel like every step towards your goal becomes its own reward. And by taking action to operationalize, our passion lets us build upon our purpose. Doing so allows your ideas to flow in a meaningful way and provides a method to gather the resources you need to help it grow into the vision you have created.

Remember that a worthy cause is a powerful movement that will attract followers. You cannot succeed alone, so take the time to invest in others and build your team to deliver results for a better future.

MEET
ADAM BOUBEDE

Adam Boubede is a coach, mentor, writer, and speaker who is passionate about inspiring people to become their best selves and leading organizations to high levels of performance. He developed this growth mindset by serving others as a Senior Enlisted Leader in the United States Air Force for over 17 years and was named one of John Maxwell's 2018 Top 100 Transformational Leaders.

Adam is also a contributor to military and industry journals, including Air Force Print News and *The Military Engineer*. He generates momentum by engaging with non-profit organizations where he works with senior leaders in government and industry and international business executives to facilitate networking events and professional development courses.

You can connect with Adam at:

www.facebook.com/adam.boubede

www.linkedin.com/in/adam-boubede

www.instagram.com/adamboubede

AN ETERNAL LIGHT

BY DENISE DURAN

I don't necessarily consider myself a religious person. And yet, so many of my pivotal memories stem from experiences growing up within my faith. When I was about four years old, my family went to Temple for a special event. What I really remember was wearing my fancy-dancy black and white hounds-tooth jacket with the fuzzy black collar, fancy-dancy socks, black patten leather Mary-Jane dress shoes, and the magnificence of the pulpit which glowed with a warm amber light.

A few months later when I began attending religious school, I looked forward to my Sundays where I'd be with friends, listening to stories, singing songs, and sometimes we'd have a 'field trip' from the school building into one of the two chapels. I'll always remember learning about the Eternal Light in synagogues reminding us of God's Eternal Presence.

Even today, I can look back and see myself as a seven or eight-year-old and feel the wonderment and fascination I had with that statement. I knew the sanctuary lights weren't always on because when school ended, I'd go to meet my mom in the courtyard of the temple. I had to go through a vestibule, which is where I'd find her waiting for me while chatting with her own friends. The sneaky kid that I was, I'd sometimes cautiously walk up to the giant doors and pull open a heavy door with my young hands to peek in, look down the long aisle to the pulpit, and then up to see if that Eternal Light was really on.

Every time, without fail, for years, no matter what time of day, or month, that Eternal Light was always aglow. It got to the point where I stopped looking for it because I knew what I'd find when I opened the door. Without realizing it, I had learned a powerful lesson in faith and trust.

My early days at the temple complimented the love and encouragement I received from my parents and extended family. My best days were at the temple. I had friends, enjoyed classwork, and was totally at peace and happy. On the flip side, my secular world was much darker.

I couldn't have been more excited to get out of kindergarten and go to 'real' school. I was primed by my parents, grandparents, and family that I was going to love school! I'd get to have fun learning and make nice friends. Within three months of beginning first grade, what I had been told was not what I was experiencing. What I ended up learning by the time I was six years old was it's bad to be smart because you get sent back to your desk, the teacher never picks your hand that's raised, and nobody wants to be your friend.

I remember, like yesterday, an assignment the class was given when I was in second grade, and I can still feel the excitement and inspiration forming in my mind, and I couldn't wait to create! If you've seen the movie *A Christmas Story,* imagine the part where Ralph comes up with the idea for his theme paper and it's the most highly regarded theme paper of all time! We were to write a poem for our mom and illustrate it. My poem included a rainbow and I used the colors of the rainbow when writing that word. I felt so proud of my work and was beaming like the rainbow I envisioned in my mind.

I can still see myself presenting Mrs. Vose my paper. She took one look at it, thrust it back at me, and spat, "That is NOT how you spell rainbow!" She turned me around, spanked my backside, and sent me back to my seat where I had to walk in front of 28 classmates looking at me. I didn't know what the word humiliated meant at seven years old, but I sure learned how it felt. As I walked home from school, hot tears streamed down my face as I finally let myself cry without anyone seeing my pain.

After that, elementary school was not a good fit, from the art teacher who felt my work belonged in the lower-left corner of the art wall to the criticism of my handwriting. I stopped turning in homework, my grades got worse, and my Eternal Light was struggling so hard to shine. Elementary school culminated in sixth grade when my parents received my state test scores by mail. They were mortified at my scores. From their perspective, they couldn't understand how in the world a bright kid could be at the bottom of the charts for the entire STATE! They did the only thing they knew how to do at the time, admonish me and made me go immediately to the school and beg my sixth-grade teacher for his help to improve my grades.

Mr. Lamb was anything but a lamb. He was a retired military man and found my carelessness and lack of organization very dishonorable. He would embarrass me in front of my classmates by dumping over my desk when he saw loose papers. He would call me out when I didn't turn in my work and make disparaging remarks that made me feel stupid, inadequate, and powerless.

While the academic element of school was bad, what really made it awful was that I had no self-esteem or confidence to make friends. I was ridiculed and felt like an outcast because, in my innocent mind, I assumed no one wanted to be friends with the loser kid.

Each year, I kept hoping, wishing, and praying that I would become a better student, that somehow I would "get it." Then the other kids would play with me, or ask me to sit with them for lunch, or pick me first or second, not last; maybe I would be invited to birthday parties. However, I was just the lazy, careless, unsatisfactory student who was consistently not meeting her potential because she's too busy day-dreaming and being in the 'Unsatisfactory' column of her report cards. My own Eternal Light was struggling so hard to shine.

RESPECT AND VALIDATION BECAME MY "REPORT CARDS".

A bright spot in the midst of my darkness was in third grade when the class was split between 3rd and 4th graders. I was daydreaming, but quickly came back to attention when the teacher began chastising the class for not knowing their multiplication tables! "HOW COULD YOU NOT KNOW THESE? THAT'S IT! YOU HAVE UNTIL TOMORROW TO LEARN YOUR MULTIPLICATION TABLES 1-10!"

As a third-grader, I thought we were responsible for knowing 1-5s. However, what I heard at that moment was that *every* student needed to know their multiplication tables 1-10 by the next day or something very, very bad was going to happen. There was *no way* I was to going to admit not knowing or asking if he meant third-graders too. Talk about a 'Firestarter!' His declaration *lit a fire* under my little day-dreamer's body, and when I got home, I lamented to my mom that I had to know all of my times-tables BY TOMORROW for a big test that I needed to pass, OR ELSE!

My mom reacted with the same terror I had, so we got busy! We figured out that 1-5s were pretty much dialed in. She explained to me how 6-10s were mastered by just putting the larger digit in front of the smaller digit. For example, she asked, "What's 4x9?" I replied, "36." "Yes," she said. "So what's 9x4?" and I responded, "36". I immediately grasped what she was teaching me. By golly, by the time I went to bed that night at 8:00, I knew that entire table from 1-10. What makes this story important? It's because it gave me something to remember and to help that light glow when it felt like there was no reason to have a light at all. The next day at school, I was able to complete the entire multiplication table test and aced it! At the age of nine years old, I learned a powerful lesson to remind me that I can accomplish anything!

Life wasn't any different in junior high except for the kids. The kids were meaner. I was already marked as a "nothing," and I was pegged as the mean-girls' kicking post. Anyone who let me hang with them during recess or lunch kind of just let me exist beside them. High school was four years of taking my destructive habits to the next level: skipping school, smoking various tobaccos, drinking, and being in demeaning relationships. I nearly failed out of high school. NO WAY was college in my future. While I attempted junior college, I found myself not going to classes, so I dropped out.

Once I started working and distancing myself from my school, I began to see that I could be successful at work. Working provided an opportunity to redefine my character as well as develop independence and even build some confidence. My light was beginning to glow a little brighter!

However, 12 years of shame, humiliation, and poor self-esteem left deep trenches in the psyche. I became a perfectionist. Respect and validation became my "report cards," which proved my value and worth. I went from being a slob to organizing like Martha Stewart. I was driven to be everything that I despised about myself growing up. It looked like I overcame my character flaws and was living life on my terms. However, if something didn't go perfectly or to plan, I felt disrespected! My critical, judging, perfectionist eyes and sharp tongue would either expose others' faults, or I'd seethe with impatience, irritation, and might even explode with frustration.

I met my husband Jamie in 1993 when my sweet little German grandmother tricked me into taking her to Friday Night Services at the Synagogue. By this time, I was sharing an apartment with a co-worker, and life was pretty fun. However, getting a Friday night request from my grandmother was always welcomed because there'd be a yummy dinner and dessert from one of our favorite restaurants. Plus, just as it did as a child, I always loved going to Services; it gave me peace, connection, and I still loved gazing at the Eternal Light.

Jamie and I married in 1997. We purchased a new home, as in newly built. We were working in San Francisco with great jobs, but I wanted more. I wanted a family. Jamie did too. However, my timeline was sooner, and of course, my needs trumped his. We welcomed our first daughter in 2000, our second daughter in 2003, and our son in 2005. By the time our son was born, we had sold our first home and moved into a new home. This one was bigger, better, and perfect!

You'd think that my Eternal Light would have been radiating! However, I was rarely satisfied. Everything had to be perfect because I'd built this belief system that said perfection equals happiness.

I remember when my eldest daughter Jackie was four years old; I know she was four because I was writing thank-you cards for those who attended her birthday party. At four years old, she was learning to read, writing her letters, and she was just a little light that shined so bright! She could write her name on her thank-you cards!

My biggest memory of that experience was getting so impatient, frustrated, and intolerant of how she was writing her name that I just took the job away from her, admonishing her for not writing her name perfectly - at four years old.

I REMEMBER WISHING I HAD A MANUAL TO HELP ME FIGURE OUT HOW TO CHANGE.

Jamie and I were about 15 years into our marriage, we had three school-aged children, and my need for perfect kids, a perfect husband, a perfect home, a perfect ME was creating an impossible home to live in and destroying our happiness. My family never wanted to rock my boat for fear of the wrath they might receive. If you had asked me if I was in fear, I would have looked at you is if you were from another planet. Fear? I wasn't afraid; I was just trying to survive! My life was spinning out of control and I needed to do something. Fear *wasn't even on my dashboard*!

I started reading self-help books. We went to family counseling, and that all helped to open my mind to different philosophies that I could use to be nicer and maintain control. However, when push came to shove, my old tendencies of criticizing, blaming, judging, intolerance, and impatience would show up. When I "lost it," it would only make me feel ashamed and remind me that I'm anything but perfect. I didn't want to behave that way, but I didn't understand how to make it stop. I remember wishing I had a manual to help me figure out how to change.

When I enrolled in the Fearless Living Institute, I had no idea that my education in becoming a life coach was going to teach me how to embrace the person I was designed to be. I learned that my demand for perfection was because I was trying to make up for all of those years and years of feeling anything but perfect. I was able to finally understand that FEAR was driving my need for perfection in order to protect my children, my husband, and yes, even me from the shame and humiliation I'd felt growing up and the label of 'Unsatisfactory' I had given myself. That manual I wished for... Guess what? I have one! And so do you; we all do! When you recognize your process, you have the knowledge to understand your unique blueprint; and that, my fire-starter friend, is a game-changer.

I do not have to live my life on a wheel that is spinning so fast because I can't keep up. You don't have to live this way either! There's a different wheel, a wheel that spins in the direction of happiness, self-acceptance, confidence, and more. Living fearlessly doesn't mean fear magically goes away. It's an invitation to lean in, be aware, and be awake to the challenge and opportunity before you. This is where your inner light can be your guide in the darkness.

Recently (2020), my 17-year-old, Carly, came home from school and told our family during dinner that a teacher reacted to a student in a way that wasn't comfortable for her. Our family talked about it at dinner, and there were opposing views on what she could do. Everyone was free to express themselves. Over the dishes, she and I talked about what she could say. We even put together an 'I' message she could use that didn't assign blame. She told me she'd think about it overnight. The next day I received a text from her saying, "I did it!" and later that evening, she showed me a message from her teacher complimenting her courage.

LIVING FEARLESSLY DOESN'T MEAN FEAR MAGICALLY GOES AWAY.

Fear is going to happen, and it doesn't want you to know this, but with it comes choice. We always have at least one choice. When you understand how you work, the choices become limitless.

What about Jackie? I asked her if she remembered the 'Thank-You Card' incident. While she didn't remember everything, she remembered me being mad. This is where being open to asking for forgiveness is truly an act of fearlessness and how our Eternal Light cannot just glow, but radiate as we combine our Eternal Light with Eternal Love.

As you explore your own journey into being a firestarter, remember our inner Light is a promise of the energy within us. Many of us have read in science journals or seen in Marvel movies that energy never goes away. That means our light is truly eternal, as in never-ending. You are never-ending, you are energy, you have power, you have a choice. You are the light designed to infuse the world with your unique purpose that will eternally illuminate the path for you and all those who benefit from the lessons, gifts, and gratitude that your journey continues to offer you.

MEET
DENISE DURAN

Denise is a Certified Fearless Living Coach (CFLC) with a private and group coaching & consulting practice. With nearly 25 years of experience in professional development, entrepreneurship, team-building, and multiple sales recognition awards, Denise's motto is practice makes progress! As a Life Coach, she's committed to creating a collaborative experience while providing life-long tools to support her clients' continued growth, creativity, and resourcefulness. Denise's gift for guiding her clients to transform their brick walls into stepping stones for success allows them to accomplish higher levels of achievement and deeper connections to themselves, including their professional and personal relationships.

Denise lives in Northern California with her husband of over twenty years. Their active life includes three children and two parents in their multi-generational home, as well as three dogs! Denise participates on several boards connected to community endeavors and when she's not coaching, with family, or serving her community, she loves spending time with friends and entertaining. She's also a fan of beach time with great books!

You are invited to connect with Denise on her website www.deniseduran. com or email her at deniseduran.tbt@gmail.com

BETTER HAS NO FINISH LINE

BY JOE BOGDAN

I was born outside of Osan Air Base, a shared American and Korean military installation located in the Republic of Korea. I never knew my father. My mother and I moved quite a few times while growing up. An unfortunate side-effect was that I never felt like I had a home, an understanding of who I was, or a family I felt that I could call my own. Growing up a latchkey child in some rough areas, on both the east and west coasts of the United States, I was surrounded by several negative influencers. Fortunately, I was also blessed enough to become close with some amazing people that I consider family to this day.

GROWING UP

Throughout my childhood, my mother struggled to maintain relationships, a stable lifestyle, and eventually, we found ourselves in financial hardship. Once I was old enough to be on my own, I felt like I needed to do something with my life. I did not believe higher education was an option for me at the time. I wasn't mature enough to stay focused and couldn't see how I could pay for it anyway. My unstable homelife left me feeling like I was on a downward spiral. So, I decided to visit the local recruiter and enlisted in the United States Air Force.

My challenging childhood provided me valuable lessons. As a latchkey child, I learned to be independent – I had no choice but to learn how to take care of myself. However, as a first-generation American, my family also ingrained in me an immense amount of pressure to succeed, which resulted in some unintended consequences. Fear of failure led to underachieving in both my academic and professional careers. Although my young military career was prospering, I feared stepping out of my comfort zone, and my personal limiting beliefs stagnated my growth, although I did not realize it at the time.

THE DEFINING MOMENT

I've had many defining moments in my life and in my career, but the one moment that had the biggest impact on me was when I took a career-broadening position at the Airman & Family Readiness Center or A&FRC. The A&FRC is the social services center found on Air Force installations. I have an engineering background by specialty, and I advanced in rank within my service rapidly because I was detail-oriented, technically adept, and an effective manager. However, I lacked some key leadership skills such as emotional intelligence, empathy, and the ability to speak in public, to name a few—skills absolutely critical to a successful assignment at the A&FRC. Quite frankly, those were critical skills for life in general.

With one phone call, a former leader of mine offered an opportunity to work at the A&FRC. This opportunity required me to leave my career field for a duration of four years, and more importantly, my comfort zone. In my head, I already turned it down. However, out of respect for him, I asked if I could think about it. I reached out to a trusted mentor, and after careful thought and a visit to the center, she advised me to take the job.

I was still not sold on the job and did not think my skills at the time would align. I was also afraid. Growing up, I had a stereotypical Asian mother who was extremely tough on me when it came to grades. When I came home with a 97% out of 100%, she would ask me what happened to the last 3%. In response, I never dared to try an advanced-placement course because bringing home a grade less than an A was simply unacceptable. This fear bled into my budding Air Force career. It resulted in me being afraid to try things when I was not 100% certain I would do well. Thus, I often underachieved while resting in my comfort zone. Luckily, my mentor did not give up on me, and because I trusted her, I took a leap of faith.

Working at the A&FRC opened a new world for me. I learned to communicate more effectively, developed resilience and the willingness to try new things, and I gained a bevy of human relations skills that made me a better leader. I also met some of the greatest people, learned how to work and lead civilian teammates, and honed my public speaking capabilities. By the end of my tour, I was comfortable teaching classes and speaking in front of a theater full of people. Most importantly, it guided me to my meaning and purpose of helping others reach their maximum potential. I believe I would not have reached the highest enlisted rank in the United States Air Force if I had not taken that opportunity. I know for sure I would not be as good a person.

MY RETURN

In late 2015, with my career-broadening assignment coming to a close, I was due to return to my career field. I felt so much angst as a lot of major changes occurred in the field while I was away. I also drew an assignment to my old stomping grounds, Osan Air Base, where the operational tempo is unforgiving. I was promoted in rank twice while at the A&FRC and was returning to a unit where I was now going to be responsible for exponentially more than I ever had been in my life. However, I was equipped with resilience skills, multiple certifications in personal and professional development, and most importantly, my meaning and purpose. But the question remained, "How do I *execute* my meaning and purpose?"

I OFTEN UNDERACHIEVED WHILE RESTING IN MY COMFORT ZONE.

Around this time, I stumbled upon a book written by someone I truly looked up to, Pete Carroll, the coach of my beloved Seattle Seahawks. In his book, *Win Forever*, Pete discusses his early failures in the National Football League. He tells the story of how much he admired Coach John Wooden, the coach of the UCLA's men's basketball team that secured 10 NCAA championships with a record seven in a row. Coach Carroll explains how he respected and admired Coach Wooden so much that after reading his book, he began to model his leadership behaviors after Wooden's.

If you know anything about Coach Carroll's first tenure in the NFL, you know that approach did not work out for him. He attributes this early failure to the fact that he did not have his own leadership philosophy—he was trying to lead like someone else versus being himself. In response, before being willing to take on another job, he took months off to dedicate himself to putting to paper his own leadership philosophy. Long story short, with his own philosophy in his hand and in his heart, he led the University of Southern California's Trojans to a 69 -12 record and two championships and also brought the city of Seattle our first and only Superbowl win.

GOOD LEADERS TEACH PEOPLE HOW TO DO; GREAT LEADERS TEACH ⹁E HOW ⹁INK.

This was when I decided it was time to solidify my own leadership philosophy. I believe that you find your leadership philosophy where your personal definition of leadership and your meaning and purpose intersect. My personal definition of leadership centers around serving others. I realized that ensuring those I was leading were armed with the resources to do their job, providing the professional and personal development they required, and instilling them with appropriate discipline, was a foundational component of my leadership philosophy.

I also realized that I found it necessary and joyful

to recognize the great things my teammates were doing, whether by tangible rewards, displaying their efforts on social media for their families to see, or by having the local public affairs office generate a story on their contributions to the mission. With Service and Recognition as the first two components, I was left with the final component of my leadership philosophy: improvement. Improving the environment in which I have influence over, the people I am blessed to lead, and myself was a natural final layer to

"BETTER HAS NO FINISH LINE" BECAME MY MANTRA.

my philosophy. It aligns with who I am as a person. This is when "Better Has No Finish Line" became my mantra. With my leadership philosophy in hand, I was prepared for my next leadership opportunity.

THE CRUCIBLE

Armed with my leadership philosophy, I landed in Osan Air Base, Republic of Korea in December of 2015. I thought I was prepared. I was wrong. Overseeing the electrical infrastructure and security systems on a base whose mission was so critical to the stability of the Korean peninsula had everyone reaching their breaking point. The harsh winters in Korea exacerbated the situation. There's cold, and then there is cold that will make you question your will as a person.

The leadership from the top down was heavily focused on mission accomplishment in my area of operations, and the lack of investment in our human capital–our people, was showing in our troops' morale and everyday demeanor. Any decent leader knows this impacts operational performance and readiness. I realized after just thirty days of boots on ground, that even I was being sucked into this whirlwind mentality of "Mission first, people when you have time." I decided to fight the urge to assimilate and bring to bear the skills I acquired while away from the career field. I decided to relentlessly execute my leadership philosophy.

When a person enters, or in my case, re-enters a tribe, they feel the pressure to conform to the norms and culture of the tribe, regardless of whether they are healthy and productive norms. It's our primal nature to do so, and in my view, the easy route. I could have easily slipped in, been a "yes man" to my leaders, and assimilated back into the culture. But how would I be honoring my mentors who gave me the opportunity, the life lessons I learned, and most importantly, the people I was entrusted to shepherd through this tough and unforgiving operational tempo? I would absolutely be failing all of them ... *and* myself. Treating people like resources to be used versus assets to be invested in is a surefire way to make your people feel unvalued. So, I looked for effective levers of change, and I focused on investing in people to ensure they felt valued.

With this in mind, I created a guiding coalition of senior enlisted leaders and developed a human-capital-investment strategy. We looked for gaps in development, we devised courses, and we executed our plan. This was in line with my leadership philosophy and we started seeing changes. Now, I won't pretend that I didn't have detractors. There were people who felt I was "overly focused" on development and not enough on the mission despite my section performing at an extremely high level. I was even told that "I was just lucky to have inherited such a good team," which I responded to with a nod and a smile.

Regardless, I did not cave to these pressures from even the most influential people around me as I was convinced it would pay dividends. It did. The morale amongst my troops was at an all-time high in an environment in which that was uncommon. To this day, I still receive messages from the members of that team and enjoy seeing them pay forward what they learned from our time together. The thing is, I learned more from them than they could have ever learned from me. They taught me that living your meaning, purpose, and leadership philosophy can bring about sparks of hope in others and in myself.

SPARKS OF HOPE

I left the crucible that is Korea with a promotion to Chief Master Sergeant, the Air Force's highest enlisted rank. I left with thicker skin from all the criticism I received during those two and a half years. But I also left with confidence in myself and in my philosophy. This experience also shaped my leadership vision.

Meaning and purpose are vital to reaching your maximum potential in life. A *leadership philosophy* is how you execute your meaning and purpose when leading. A *leadership vision* is what keeps you on track. I discovered after coming out on the other side of that crucible stronger and validated that the vision I wanted to live was to develop world-championship-winning coaching trees. Good leaders teach people how to do; great leaders teach people how to think – not how to think like them, but to develop their own frameworks to engage life and the challenges they may face. I realized that the legacy I wanted to leave behind is a long line of coaches who can "win" in life.

Many see people who are successful and assume they've reached that level of success overnight. As you can see, this truncated version of my story had a lot of ups and downs, successes and failures, and everything in between. So, in an effort to live out my vision of developing world-championship-winning coaching trees, I've captured some of the lessons I've learned along the way and share them with you here.

Stretch outside your comfort zone: Doing your best at something you want to do or at something you know you are good at is ordinary. It takes character and courage to step outside your comfort zone and put maximum effort into something you don't want to do. I lived in my comfort zone, and it limited me in ways I could not comprehend. When I stepped out, my life truly began. Fight the urge to play it safe and see the challenge in front of you as an opportunity to become better…not something you fear to fail.

Meaning and Purpose: Reflect on your purpose and meaning. The great Viktor Frankl explained that we all have a will to meaning. Sometimes finding it can be challenging, but asking yourself some simple, but difficult questions can be a great start. What matters to you? What brings you joy? When do you feel energized versus drained? These questions can help identify what you are "meant" to do.

Develop your own leadership philosophy: Meaning and purpose are not enough. You must find the vehicle in which you will execute that meaning and purpose. In leadership, this is your leadership philosophy. Leadership does not have to come in the form of leading a business or military unit. It can be leading your family, or at minimum yourself. There is no off-button to leadership. So how do you lead? Identifying your core values and aligning them to an actionable plan is a good start on developing your leadership philosophy and, eventually, your vision.

Embrace your amazing: Take the more difficult route and fight the urge to assimilate. We don't need leaders that are just products of their environment. We need DISRUPTERS! Embrace your special traits, attributes, and the skills you have gained along the way, and share them. Help make us all better!

I live my purpose and meaning, my philosophy, and my personal vision statement in so many ways today. I have the honor of leading and coaching almost 500 Airmen in the ultimate goal of defending our Constitution and our Nation's interests. I help produce winning coaches as a professor of leadership studies. When I discovered and accepted who I was, I realized that I could change the world, one person at a time. You can do the same.

MEET
JOE BOGDAN

Joseph "Joe" Bogdan is a Senior Enlisted Leader in the United States Air Force with more than 20 years of service. He is currently the Chief Enlisted Manager for almost 500 military and civilian engineers at Travis Air Force Base in California. In this capacity, he is responsible for leading, organizing, training, and equipping members to execute missions at home station and abroad.

He has a wide array of leadership experience in the engineering, communications, and social services career fields and has employed his skills at multiple assignments across the globe. Driven by his passion for helping others reach their professional and personal goals, he continues to be a mentor to hundreds and is a sought-after speaker and instructor on a variety of topics to include resilience, management, and leadership.

He holds instructional certifications in multiple courses to include Franklin Covey's The 7 Habits of Highly Effective People, Shipley Communications' Four Lenses and is a Master Resiliency Trainer certified at The University of Pennsylvania. He holds an undergraduate degree in Social Sciences with a minor in Homeland Security from the University of Maryland University College and earned his graduate degree in Organizational Leadership at Brandman University, where he is currently an adjunct professor of both undergraduate and graduate leadership studies.

Joe is also a co-founder of the Llama Leadership website and a host of the Llama Lounge podcast that explores topics on all things life, learning, and leadership. You can reach out to Joe at the Llama Leadership website at www.llamaleadership.com, on his LinkedIn page at https://www.linkedin.com/in/jybogdan/, or by email at llamaleadership@gmail.com.

BE THE CHANGE

BY ALBA CORDERO SOTO

My journey and experience with trauma started at the tender age of three. I was born in the Dominican Republic, but at the age of five, I was a delicate rose that was uprooted from her homeland and placed in the concrete jungle of Brockton, Massachusetts, in the middle of winter. It was January of 1995. There was this marvel look in my eyes as I saw that everything was covered in white, yet I felt like I was frozen – shocked by the cold air and my suspended breath. Just a little girl, I was scared, yet I was filled with hope as I looked up at my father, my protector, my savior.

I had lived my life up until then without my father. It was just my mom, my brother, and me. For whatever reason, when I met my father for the first time, I fell in love and I knew I would go to the ends of the Earth to be with him. In Brockton, I lived with my father, stepmother, and five siblings in a small apartment building where we were two per room. The house in which my dad lived in the Dominican Republic felt like a mansion compared to this, but I didn't care because I had my father, my protector.

It was at this time that I began my first addiction, people-pleasing. I would do anything for my father's approval. I needed to be seen as a "good girl" because deep down I felt the opposite. My father was very much emotionally unavailable, and while he provided and was

I KNOW THAT THE GREATER THE FIRE, THE GREATER THE TRANSFORMATION.

there physically, he wouldn't show love. However, that didn't matter to me because he saved me.

All that is done in the dark comes to light. That once delicate flower had adapted to her new environment, and I was blossoming. Four years had passed before my darkness reappeared. I remember it like it was yesterday. I was nine years old, and until then, I had forgotten what had happened to me. I heard laughter and adult conversations in the living room. I had no idea who had come over to visit and knew better than to insert myself into adult conversations. Then, my father called me in the room and said, "Come and greet your uncle. He just arrived from the Dominican Republic."

So, I went in with my usual happy-go-lucky self … and he gave me this sly smile. With this sly smile, he impregnated me with guilt as my body remembered what he had done to me. At the time, I did not remember the details of my molestation or what it even meant. My body tensed up, and I looked down at the floor in shame. But no one seemed to notice. My father questioned, "What are you waiting for? Aren't you gonna say hello to your uncle?" My dad spoke to me in Spanish, and I knew that when he said, "Saludalo" (greet him), he meant I had to open up my arms, hug him, and kiss him on the cheek and say, "Bendicion, Tio." "Bendicion, Tio" is a term of respect and endearment; its exact translation is "Blessings, Uncle" and this is something that we Dominicans traditionally say for greetings and farewells along with a hug and a kiss on the cheek. At that very moment, I felt naked and exposed to everyone in the room, so I walked away at the first opportunity with hopes to get rid of this knot in my stomach and the filth that took over my body.

That night, I struggled to fall asleep, and when I eventually did, I began to have flashbacks. I was in the bathroom at my grandmother's house with him. There he was with that smile again and the look of desire. Picture … Picture …Picture … I woke up out of my sleep and I was relieved to be alone in my bed, but my heart was racing yet tingling with desire. I laid there confused, but mostly ashamed. I asked myself how I could think such provocative thoughts and what was this tingling feeling I felt between my legs. I tried to make sense of it and in my egocentric mind, I just knew that it was my fault that I had attracted this and that I was guilty.

I BEGAN MY FIRST ADDICTION, PEOPLE-PLEASING.

From that day forward, I just knew that everyone could see me being guilty of doing unthinkable acts and even worse with a family member. I was completely out of control as I allowed my thoughts to possess me, and every day when I got dressed, I wore my guilt like it was never going out of style. As a rose, I began to wither and face the floor.

It was at that same age that I discovered my second addiction: self-soothing behaviors, also known as masturbation. These memories and these thoughts were with me, and they had become a part of me so much that I felt out of control. The relief that I felt would give me back control of my body and then fill me with even more guilt and shame. It was a recurring cycle. The memory took over my identity and made me feel out of control. Masturbation gave me a sense of pleasure and control that never lasted. I turned to addiction to cope with the deep shame that I felt, and in exchange, my shame grew more as it confirmed the narrative that this was all my fault.

The flashbacks became a movie that would replay in my mind most nights as I fell asleep. I realized it wasn't just my uncle. It was many cousins as well. The days where I was safe and away from those who violated me were over. One by one, they were coming to the United States, and my life turned into a war zone. With each knock at the door and new visitor, I did not know if I would be presented with a land mine that would ignite these buried memories inside

I ALLOWED MY THOUGHTS TO POSSESS ME.

of me. At times, the sly smile would give it away, and sometimes it would be the long and tight embrace, and other times it would be the provocative caress that would bring me back.

I was not born to be the brightest or the tallest-stemmed rose in the garden, yet my resilience allowed me to overcome. My inability to speak my truth and find my voice meant I lived a lie, and as a result, family identified me as a liar. My fear of rejection and need to please meant that I could not be myself, and every day I would wake up trying to be what I thought the world wanted me to be.

As a teen, I continued to lean into my coping skill of people-pleasing by excelling in school. My desire to please my father took many forms and turns. My father would say that he wanted me to be a lawyer; I would wake up and start announcing that I was going to become a lawyer. Then, my father would turn around and say that lawyers were liars, cheaters, and thieves. All of a sudden, I did not want to be a lawyer anymore. He then would say that he wanted one of his children to be a doctor, so next thing you know, I was announcing that I wanted to be a pediatrician. After my father and I watched the movie "Million Dollar Baby," a story of a boxer that fought her way to fame and riches, my father was convinced that I would be the next million dollar baby and that his daughter would share a ring with the infamous Laila Ali. To no surprise, I expressed interest in boxing, and within a week, I was training at a local gym.

Through boxing, I was able to release my aggression while making my father proud. My father was front and center at all of my fights, and he was by far the loudest, especially when I got my first TKO (technical knockout) during my third fight. I was on a high like no other, and I was undefeated 8-0 with 1 TKO. Those were some of the best memories of my life. I went from #metoo to #neveragain.

For years, I was surrounded by people, but I had this internal loneliness. I could be in a room of people and feel lonely, and I convinced myself that I needed to be around people to cover up the inner voice that told me I was not good enough. One day while commuting three hours to and from work, I considered this to be a forced opportunity where I challenged myself to resist picking up the phone to drown out my inner dialogue. I quickly realized what I was running away from my whole life; my inner voice was like a broken record that was stuck on, not feeling worthy, and not feeling deserving. I knew that my road to recovery from being addicted to pleasing people was going to be a long, unpaved path, yet my spirit told me that I could not continue this fight or flight relationship I had with myself.

As I reconnected with my inner being, I realized that my value came from my relationship with God, not from that of man. The moment I surrendered to my inner being, I began living. While on this journey, I bumped into my authentic self. I had been in my people-pleasing state for almost 30 years, and it was as if I was being introduced to myself for the first time. Running away was not an option. Distractions were no longer necessary as I began to build a loving relationship with myself. One by one, I began to take off the masks, starting with the mask that told me that I needed to smile though my heart was breaking. Each of my masks had served a purpose and had allowed me to survive up to that point, so I said thank you and farewell. I knew I wanted more from life.

While my journey of self-discovery will last forever, I can now answer the questions: Who am I? Whose am I? Who am I called to be? I am a positive, resilient, and a radiant rose. My roots are firmly planted by a stream of God's everlasting love. The thorns of my past do not limit my growth; instead, they represent my resilience. For I am not my past, I am the soul that lives within.

"The fire of your suffering will become the light of your consciousness."
-Eckhart Tolle

I know that the greater the fire, the greater the transformation. Trauma has been my greatest teacher, and now I am sharing the tools that I have learned with the world. I am the change that I have been looking for.

For as long as I could remember, I have helped others with my intuitive wisdom and have always been referred to as an old soul. As a certified trauma life coach, transformational speaker, and author, I am sharing the tools and strategies that have liberated me from my trauma.

TIPS TO OVERCOME TRAUMA

Ask for help! If you are experiencing thoughts of harming yourself, contact the National Suicide Prevention Hotline at 1-800-273-8255.

Speak up! Reclaim your voice by speaking your truth. If you are not ready to talk to someone, begin journaling.

Join a community - There are many communities that can help provide support, such as support groups, women empowerment groups, and even some religious communities.

Read - There are so many memoirs and self-help books that can provide wisdom and healing.

Attend therapy - Find a therapist that specializes in trauma. EMDR (Eye Movement Desensitization and Reprocessing) Therapy is a special form of therapy that supports trauma healing without the need to talk about it.

Get reiki treatment - Energy healing can help to resolve energy blocks caused by sexual trauma and years of silence.

Music/Art Therapy - Creative energy can help with expression in ways that are very relaxing.

Get a Life Coach - A life coach, particularly one who specializes in trauma, is someone that could help you as you embark on your healing journey.

Move Your Body - Yoga and exercise can help you reconnect with your body again.

Breathe - Silence is helpful to connect with your inner being. Prayer and meditation are great ways to interact with God and your higher self.

MEET
ALBA CORDERO SOTO

Alba Cordero Soto is a certified trauma life coach, transformational speaker, author, reiki practitioner, podcast host, and nurse supervisor at a Harm Reduction Clinic within a community health center. As the visionary and founder of Alba Soto TLC, her mission is to support sexual trauma survivors on their healing journey and help them find their voice and reclaim their power. As a survivor herself, she shares the lessons that allowed her to break the shackles of sexual trauma and heal for generations to come.

Soto is dedicated to helping teen girls and single mothers who have suffered from sexual trauma. As a bilingual, Spanish-speaking, certified trauma life coach, she teaches that, "Without tools, trauma Rules."

Soto's vision is to create a community of resilient women and teens through her sisters' circle community, "Better TogetHER," a sacred space to connect with other like-spirited, resilient women who are ready to move towards a life that is free of shame, guilt, and anger.

She is also the proud mother of four and counting, wife, and entrepreneur.

You are invited to connect with Alba on her website www.albasototlc.com or albasototlc@gmail.com

OUT OF THE DARKNESS

DAVID BENNETT

When I was younger, maybe 12 to 13 years old, I discovered a fire burning deep within my soul. The fire, for me, represents the best part of who I am. Stuff like feelings of love, passion, purpose, desire, action, determination, hope, faith, trust, gut feelings, butterflies, God, and the Universe's vibration.

You know, the stuff you can't see, but you know it is there. That is the fire. The fire represents all of those things.

Living on Earth for 30 years now, I have noticed a few things about this "fire" that I want to express. It can glow red hot, and when it does, oh boy, do you feel it's truly alive. It can also be a very dim light that flickers like a candle in the wind.

When your life is like this, it seems like a cloud of darkness surrounds your whole life. Whether it is a red-hot flame or small, dim candlelight, we all have this fire deep inside us. However, the darkness is something I want you to be aware of because it is within us. The darkness only has one thing in mind, one goal. Its purpose is to SNUFF THE FIRE OUT. It wants to DESTROY THE LIGHT.

You see, the darkness knows that if your fire burns hot enough and your light shines bright enough, it can spread. And if it spreads, there will be too much light, and the darkness won't have a place to be. The darkness doesn't want this.

It represents hopelessness, shame, stress, anxiety, past mistakes, failures, hardships, ALL OF IT. The darkness hates your fire and your light. It wants to make that fire that burns deep down inside of you so dim that it has no chance of spreading. It wants to overpower you. It wants to consume you. It wants to convince you that there is no hope, there is no light at the end of the tunnel, and it wants you to believe that your life is over.

Do you know what I mean? Have you ever been in such a dark moment of your life that you didn't see a way out? I bet when you were in that moment, or maybe you're living this in the current moment, you were overwhelmed by all of this darkness.

The question is, HOW DO YOU GET OUT? Ladies and gentleman, if you are in this moment right now; if you are struggling to see a future when you feel there is no path or guide to that said future; if you are feeling lost in all this darkness, please hear my voice right now. Listen to me carefully.

Stop what you are doing right now and take a deep breath.

Hold it for three seconds. [breathe in]

> YOU SEE, THE DARKNESS KNOWS THAT IF YOUR FIRE BURNS HOT ENOUGH AND YOUR LIGHT SHINES BRIGHT ENOUGH, IT CAN SPREAD.

Now, let it out. [breathe out]

It's time. Right now is the time. No longer are you going to be controlled by this darkness! No longer are you going to be living with regrets! No longer are you going to live in your shame! It's time to reach deep down inside of you, down into the core of who you are, and start feeding your fire.

There is a beautiful light on the inside of you that the darkness is scared to let shine. It's time to let the light shine again. Your fire, your light, and yourself are going to get better. It's time to pull

YOU out of this darkness.

Dig Deep ... as far as you can go ... and look your darkness in the eyes. It would help if you faced this HEAD-ON. DON'T you DARE LOOK AWAY! Look at it in the eyes.

Then say this with all of your heart and soul: "I no longer need you. I am no longer allowing you to control me. You will not thrive off me anymore. You will not survive here. Today, right now, is your eviction notice."

Make sure you STAND FIRM, ladies and gentlemen! It will do everything to fight you and use all of its power to convince you that it's more significant than you are, and you are nothing. But keep fanning your flames. Keep standing firm. Keep shining your light as bright as you can.

Take action, take ownership of your life, and drown out that darkness! Find people that will help you fan your flames. It would be best if you started spreading your fire and your light. Connect with people. Create a bonfire community.

Because, like it or not, you will eventually become a reflection of the company you keep. Therefore, you might as well find people who will fan your flames rather than people who want to smother it. Choose yourself first and stop wasting time around things that don't feed you.

Dig deep and find what your spirit wants you to be. What makes you come to life? Some people call this your purpose. Some people call it your gift. You choose what you want it to be. I call it my gift. Most importantly, I know that my gift engulfs my burning flame. Proverbs 18:16 states, "A man's gift makes room for him and brings him before great men." Another translation says, "A man's gift opens doors for him and brings him before great men."

FIND PEOPLE THAT WILL HELP YOU FAN YOUR FLAMES.

If you reach deep down into yourself and discover what lights you up, it will make way for you in this world. I truly believe this with all my heart. Not even six months ago, that cloud of darkness surrounded me as well. I was broke, alone, and almost homeless. Truthfully, it was hard to see a way out. But I did what I am telling you today. I dug deep. I looked my darkness in the eyes and demanded, "Move! You are in my way! You don't belong here! TODAY IS YOUR EVICTION NOTICE!"

I discovered way back at age 19 that I loved to speak and help motivate people because I understood that we all have tough days. It wasn't until I was 29 years old, when I stopped letting the darkness control me and I started using my gift and living my purpose, that I took control. This #FIRESTARTER book is living proof that if you look darkness in the eyes and follow your gift, anything is possible. I am so grateful I could look my darkness in the eyes and say, "GET OUT."

If I didn't, I would hate to know where I would be right now. By evicting my darkness, it helped me find my gift. My gift helped me create the "I Needed This" podcast. I found an outlet for me to speak my truth.

Just like the Bible verse promised, it has opened doors for me. It has made way for me. In fact, because of my podcast, I was asked to be a part of this book. NONE OF THIS would have occurred if I hadn't looked my darkness in the eyes and spoken the shift into my life. It would have never happened. I had to take action, choose myself first, and fan my flames until they burned hot.

What seemed like a very dim light six months ago is now a full-on burning fire that is starting to spread. A wildfire is breaking out, and my goal is to spark something in you.

I WANT YOU TO PULL YOURSELF OUT OF THIS DARKNESS.

I WANT YOU TO TAKE A STEP, DIG DEEP, AND FAN YOUR FLAME.

MAKE YOUR LIGHT SHINE AGAIN.

I promise you! NO! I guarantee you that you won't regret it if you do what you have been holding yourself back from all these years. It is time, ladies and gentlemen, to start allowing yourself to be happy again. Remember, it is going to take time, but keep fanning those flames. The hotter and brighter you get, the better the chances of attracting other lights.

More fire is good. The brighter we are, the hotter we are, the less power the darkness has. You can kill it. But it is up to you. You got this. Keep moving. Keep being persistent.

You WILL WIN.

It's time to pull yourself out of the darkness!

MEET
DAVID BENNETT

David Bennett discovered his passion for being a positive change when he was at a very young age. He is known for his optimistic attitude and positive outlook on life. After attending a purpose and passion seminar in 2018, he had a life-changing revelation. It inspired him to become a certified life coach with the school, "The Academy of Modern Applied Psychology."

Now, David is a Certified Life Purpose Coach, Motivational Podcaster, Teacher, and Motivational Speaker. You might know him as the host of the "I Needed This" podcast, the face of the "I Needed This Dave" YouTube channel, or heard him speak at one of your events! Currently, David teaches people how to discover their own purpose and passion with his three-step program called "The Lion Within."

David tries to live up to his purpose and passion statement every day, which is: "With Motivation, Desire, and a whole lot of action, I challenge myself and others to release that 'Fire' that's inside all of us. Take action and be the change you want to see in the world. So that by the end of the day, we can all say we were our best selves."

You can reach out to David and find more resources about him at:

www.INeededThisDave.com or ineededthisdave@gmail.com

LIFE TEACHES WHEN WE LISTEN

BY MOUSSA MIKHAIL

Growing up as an adolescent in American culture usually carries a certain level of stress and challenges regardless of who you are. Oftentimes, we don't recognize how these challenges affect our programming as adults in our personal lives and relationships. During my childhood in Las Vegas, I witnessed gang violence, poverty, and homelessness, but one of the greatest challenges I faced was at home with my parents. They never truly had a loving relationship.

Experiencing verbal abuse and constant anger as a child led to some psychological programming that I unknowingly adopted. My parents were going through foreclosure on our home during my last year of middle school, and this led to an unsightly divorce. My father, two brothers, and I relocated to the east coast in New Jersey, where I started my high school journey.

I used football as my outlet during this time, and it helped distract me from dealing with the dysfunctionality of my family and the sadness I felt being without my mom. Football was my life as a child, so it was natural for me to use it as my method of solace and expression. Having left everyone I knew behind, I started building strong relationships through football until I had to move to another high school following my freshman football season.

Another change of pace and adjustment was overwhelming for me. I decided to just focus all my energy on football. This was helpful; I noticed when I focused all my energy on one thing, it depleted my ability to show up everywhere else. But I was passionate about it, so I didn't even notice it was affecting my grades. I didn't even notice I wasn't dealing with emotional issues because I felt I was good at masking everything I was truly feeling while playing the sport I loved. This habit of not being self-aware or expressing myself was unhealthy. I did not realize it was actually taking away the vitality in my life.

This internal dysfunction haunted me for many years to come. During my sophomore year in high school, I had a tumor in my knee that was hindering my ability to play, and I ended up having it surgically removed on my 15th birthday. This set me back athletically.

After that year was over, I ended up training like a maniac because I wanted to be a great athlete again. I trained for hours daily. My body couldn't handle the amount of brute-force training I was putting it through. I was planning to be a starter for a championship varsity football team.

That was my sole focus. My junior year became the toughest for me. I had overworked my body and developed a stress fracture in my hip. There was no way I could continue to play in that kind of physical shape, and definitely not at the level I was aspiring to play. This was a damaging blow because football was the world to me. I was playing through the pain for a long time without understanding it was just getting worse and worse. I should have realized there was a serious issue when I had to take 4-6 ibuprofen pills a night so I could actually sleep and be able to walk the next day.

I didn't think it would get worse than that, but it did. I developed the same tumor that I had previously on my knee again. I realized it might be a sign that I needed to give up my biggest passion and dream. As this was going on, my father was diagnosed with lung cancer. Amongst all the other changes that one cannot truly prepare for, this was an unexpected blow to my emotional stability. I again believed I was strong by not displaying my emotions, and being what I felt at the time was stoic. This was when I made the hardest decision of my life. I gave up football to get a job to support myself and my family.

Towards the end of my junior year, I still wanted to be a part of something larger – a team that had a mission greater than myself. This feeling of lack nudged me to look into different avenues of the military and what I wanted to accomplish outside of high school. I decided that I wanted to become an FBI agent and join the Navy to help me stand out versus the average college graduate. I needed to get away from New Jersey and begin a new journey, and the Navy fit my idea of that.

Before my senior year, my father passed away from cancer. Most people didn't even know about it because I didn't announce it to the world. Again, I held it all in and didn't allow myself to receive much-needed support. I really kept to myself in high school, and his death was definitely a huge challenge for me. After this blow, I began developing resilience to pain. A resilience that, if not checked, can lead to numbing and an inability to feel love and empathy. I put on armor constantly, which was eliminating any vulnerability on my part. I felt that if I just didn't open up to anyone, I would be protected from actually dealing with the emotional pain. In reality, I was causing the very pain I intended to protect. What we resist persists. By holding on to the massive amount of armor blocking in light, love, and support from others to enter my heart, it simultaneously prevented my light from shining outwardly. It wasn't until after my military career that I noticed this was not only affecting my ability

I DIDN'T EVEN NOTICE I WASN'T DEALING WITH EMOTIONAL ISSUES BECAUSE I FELT I WAS GOOD AT MASKING EVERYTHING.

to have quality relationships but it was impacting my health. We must reflect and look at the lesson in all things to enable our capability of interrupting the patterns that sabotage our entire lives if unchecked. All obstacles we face shape us for our purpose if we allow ourselves to view them as an opportunity to become a better version of ourselves.

The Navy was my next journey. I believed I had it all planned out after high school. I truly believed I was going to get a top-secret clearance in the Navy, military experience, training, a degree, and become an FBI special agent. This was my personal path to living a happy, successful life. Even though this was a great plan for a 17-year-old, it did not take into account my true dreams. It accounted for what I felt was the best, most attainable path for me.

The Navy was my choice because of all the traveling and uniqueness of being on a ship, and being a part of the global presence of the US Navy. I knew that out of all the avenues I could choose within the Navy, there was one that I was adamant about not pursuing–submarine duty. When I arrived at the Military Entrance Processing Station in Brooklyn, NY, I completed all the necessary exams and physicals. This all-day event ended with me selecting my rate, the Navy term for "job." The recruiters at the facility explained that I wouldn't qualify for the intelligence rate I wanted because my parents were not born in America. Even though this information was completely false, I believed it and was very heartbroken. This news threw off my intentions for getting the one thing I felt that would make me stand out the most for becoming an FBI agent.

I STILL WANTED TO BE A PART OF SOMETHING LARGER – A TEAM THAT HAD A MISSION GREATER THAN MYSELF.

They came back with two rates to choose from, Submarine Machinist Mate, which is simply a

Submarine Mechanic, and the Submarine Electronics Computer Field. I was enraged about this because I emphasized that I did not want submarine duty. In reality, I was just frightened by the thought of spending weeks and months at a time in a tube submerged underwater without sunlight, internet, and the simple joys of life. I wanted an intelligence job because I felt I was keeping the end in mind, which I know now was a strong trait to have when planning and envisioning.

I agitatedly pleaded that I needed to have another rate with a clearance. I asked to come back another day, knowing I would have to retake all the exams and physicals. My recruiter insisted I should pick one, and I could request to change it in the seven-month period I would be waiting to ship out to boot camp. I signed a five-year contract with what I considered the most uncomfortable rate in the Navy–Submarine Electronics Computer Field. I was exasperated, extremely worried, and anxious. I thought I was making a huge mistake and had no certainty of what to expect anymore. I needed some advice and comfort. I knew submariners get at least a secret clearance instead of the highest–top-secret, which I felt would still be an advantage against anyone who did not possess any. I reached out to a friend and mentor, Nick Zirpoli, who was already in the navy for several years by that time. I explained how I was fully opposed to the idea of being on a submarine and needed to change my rate. He empathized when I reached out about the two rates I was given as my final fate for the Navy. The Navy has a saying, "Choose your rate, choose your fate."

My mentor knew several submariners that he worked closely with and saw a distinct difference between the submariners and non-submariners. Submarine crews are smaller compared to the rest of the navy, but the workload isn't proportionate. They

"NO MATTER WHAT PATH YOU CHOSE, THE EXPERIENCE WILL BE WHAT YOU MAKE OF IT.

had a different work ethic due to the circumstances in which they have to live and work. They have to spend weeks and months underwater at a time, cut off from the world in less than desirable living conditions. Most of the crew has to share the racks or "beds." Three sailors are assigned to two racks. This is known as "hot-racking" due to the fact we would get into the rack shortly after someone has awakened to relieve the watch. Along with this, submarines have a really high operation tempo, which keeps them extremely busy in preparation for the next task or mission.

Submarines are highly technical pieces of equipment that have all the necessary tools to keep us alive and submerged safely with only 130-150 crew members. Larger ships can have hundreds to thousands of crew members. Nick gave me advice that I would cherish forever. When I was distraught about this decision, he said, "No matter what path you choose, the experience will be what you make of it. The experience will be made up of your positive outlook, the people you meet, and how far you push yourself to be better and advance. Keep with the successful crowd, get your education, look good in uniform, show up on time, give your best, and have fun."

That was exactly what I needed to hear at that moment. It immediately made sense to me and became the most pivotal moment of my life. In reflection, I was guided to meet Nick when he walked into the Best Buy where I worked one evening in uniform after he got off work. I immediately felt called to talk to him about the Navy. He was instrumental in getting me to decide what I wanted to do and in teaching me the most important lesson that I never forgot throughout my naval career and my life.

I was just afraid of getting out of my comfort zone, but Nick's words empowered me to look at the situation through a completely different paradigm. It is the paradigm I now choose to study every aspect of my life. No matter where I am or what I am doing, the experience will be what I make of it. I can go on the submarine scared and hate it, expecting to be miserable five years of my life, or I can make it the best five years of my life where I learn more about myself, others, leadership, and life. I can make it an experience that empowers me to do all things I have my eyes set on. I can use this experience to strengthen my mind and faith.

I learned that day that I have control over my experience in life. I can make it beautiful or ugly, based on my perception of it. I decided to go for the submarine life and push myself out of my comfort zone. I had no idea what to truly expect. Submarine operations are top secret, so I could not just google how my experience would be or get a strong understanding of what I was about to get into. However, I felt like meeting Nick was not a coincidence. I felt like everything that was happening to me was a lesson.

I realized I was trying to control my outcome. It is always good to have a plan, but even with a plan we have no control over certain aspects of our lives. I learned at this young age that I needed to surrender. I believe everything happens for a reason, and all challenges are there to shape me to become who I need to be in order to fulfill my purpose. There is no such thing as a perfect journey. It is about how we choose to make that journey and our attitude towards it. Perfection lies within the imperfections.

I was stationed in Pearl Harbor, HI on the Fast Attack Submarine USS Columbia where I completed three deployments and countless underways (the military term for being out to sea) to support the operations that were slated for us. I got a strong taste of what it was like to serve and work innumerable hours. On my second six-month deployment, I had another pivotal moment.

I realized I was not going to pursue any government or federal job when I got out. I did not want to work innumerable hours my whole life. I had a vision of becoming a speaker, writer, and podcast host. My heart was calling me in a completely different direction. I felt out of alignment with myself in the military. I developed a new plan for myself post-Navy.

When I got out of the Navy, I decided I wanted my realtor license in my hometown of Las Vegas and immersed myself in real estate. I believed I should work on getting financially free, so I could work on my dreams without any financial burden. After getting my license in real estate and working it my first year out of the military, I still felt out of alignment. That is when I realized I had it all backward. I wanted to become financially free first and then work on my dream. In reality, I needed to work on my dream until I was financially free.

I realized that more important than finances, was living a life congruent with my purpose and being in alignment with who I want and need to be to become a person of impact. I discovered if I am living fully, money is not going to be an issue. I decided to surrender to my dream and focus all my attention on becoming the podcaster, speaker, and writer that my heart was calling upon. The words of Theodore Roosevelt rung in my head, "Do what you can, with what you have, where you are." The hardest part is always starting, but it became a must for me to fulfill my purpose. We must eradicate the limiting beliefs that prevent us from starting on our dream. If it is in our heart, then we are equipped to accomplish it. Not only are we equipped, but it is also our responsibility to give all that we are. If we are not, we are preventing the world from receiving the gift of our authentic self.

I have seen too many people stay in the military or their jobs because of fear – fear of the unknown, fear of failure, and fear of making a mistake. Whatever the fears are, the pleasure of achieving your dreams and living a heart-centered life congruent with who you really are is much greater than the fear. To become all we are meant to become, we must submit ourselves. We must go into the unknown and trust that we have all we need to let our gift be received fully by the world. Do not let the resistance prevent you from living the life you dream of and what your heart is calling you to live. You deserve it. You are worthy.

MEET
MOUSSA MIKHAIL

Moussa Mikhail was born August 10, 1996, of Christian-Egyptian immigrant parents in the City of Lights–Las Vegas, Nevada. Following high school athletics and submarine life in the Navy, he landed back in Las Vegas, NV working in real estate.

Moussa's passion and dedication to reading for self-improvement not only improved his military advancement, but gave him a better way of thinking about life and success. It also helped him discover his entrepreneurial spirit.

Moussa invested heavily in learning about the mind, body, leadership, business, and real estate. It led him to get his real estate license and start a credit repair/financial services business in order to become self-employed after leaving the Navy. More importantly, it led him to his passion for podcasting, writing, speaking, and coaching.

Moussa now shares his passion for life's journey and the creation of a strong community around self-mastery through his podcast: *The Conqueror Approach. A podcast on self-mastery.* To hear more, subscribe wherever you listen to podcasts and visit www.MoussaMikhail.com.

CONCLUSION

It doesn't matter where you've come in contact with fire – in nature, in a fireplace, industrial flames, or just a simple match – the heat is memorable. No matter where the heat is applied, the heat causes change. The elements of fire always serve as that catalyst. Metals become malleable or liquify. Wood turns into carbon. Food heats up and cooks. There is always an effect.

The most relevant part? You cannot be affected by the fire and walk away saying the fire never happened. Once you have been exposed, the memory is there permanently.

It's no different than your experience as a reader of *#FIRESTARTERS*. You cannot walk away from this experience saying the fire never happened. You will not be able to say that you haven't been motivated, inspired, and spurred to change.

These men and women have presented truth, motivation, and fuel for cataclysmic excellence in your leadership and in your life.

The best way for you to begin sharing what these stories have meant to you is to visit our website at www.firestartersbookproject.com or email us at info@firestartersbookproject.com. We look forward to hearing from you!

JOIN THE #FIRESTARTERS MOVEMENT TODAY!

- Are you a solopreneur, podcaster, coach, speaker, or founder of a non-profit?

- Are you ready to level up by collaborating with a community of creative thought leaders?

- Do you have a compelling testimony that you want to share with the world?

- Have you wanted to write a book or have been told that you should, and the thought of writing a "whole" book feels overwhelming?

**You now have the opportunity to become
a published author in future collections!**

The #FIRESTARTERS Book Project is a co-authoring opportunity to join forces with creative thought leaders, like yourself. With this opportunity, you receive so many priceless perks that are unheard of in other co-author book programs. These perks help you level up your brand for your business or non-profit, your podcast, your mastermind group, whatever it is that makes up you!

**For more details, visit www.firestartersbookproject.com
to schedule your consultation today!**

We offer a limited number of co-author slots per collection. Act now!

We are looking forward to collaborating with you!

We have so much to gain when we join forces!

WE ARE READY TO GET YOU FIRED UP!

Made in the USA
Monee, IL
16 July 2021